Friedrich Hechelmann

# Mystic Gateways



Bluestar Communications
Woodside, California

For information write to:
Bluestar Communications
44 Bear Glenn
Woodside, CA. 94062
1-800-6-BLUESTAR

First printing 1995

ISBN: 1-885394-11-x



Printed in Hong Kong

# Friedrich Hechelmann

Friedrich Hechelmann was born in 1948 in Isny, Germany. He studied at *Akademie der Bildenden Künste* in Vienna as a Master Scholar of Rudolf Hausner. In 1972, he received the award of the Wiener Akademie and completed his first exhibition in Vienna.

Since then he has had numerous exhibitions world wide. He has also worked as a director for German Television, was responsible for the stage sets for many operas and has illustrated several books.

He is one of the most well-known living artists in Europe today.

**The images contained in this book are also available as Postable Art™ cards.**

For a free full color catalog of art by
Friedrich Hechelmann and other selected artists contact:

Bluestar Communications
44 Bear Glenn
Woodside, CA. 94062
1-800-6-BLUESTAR

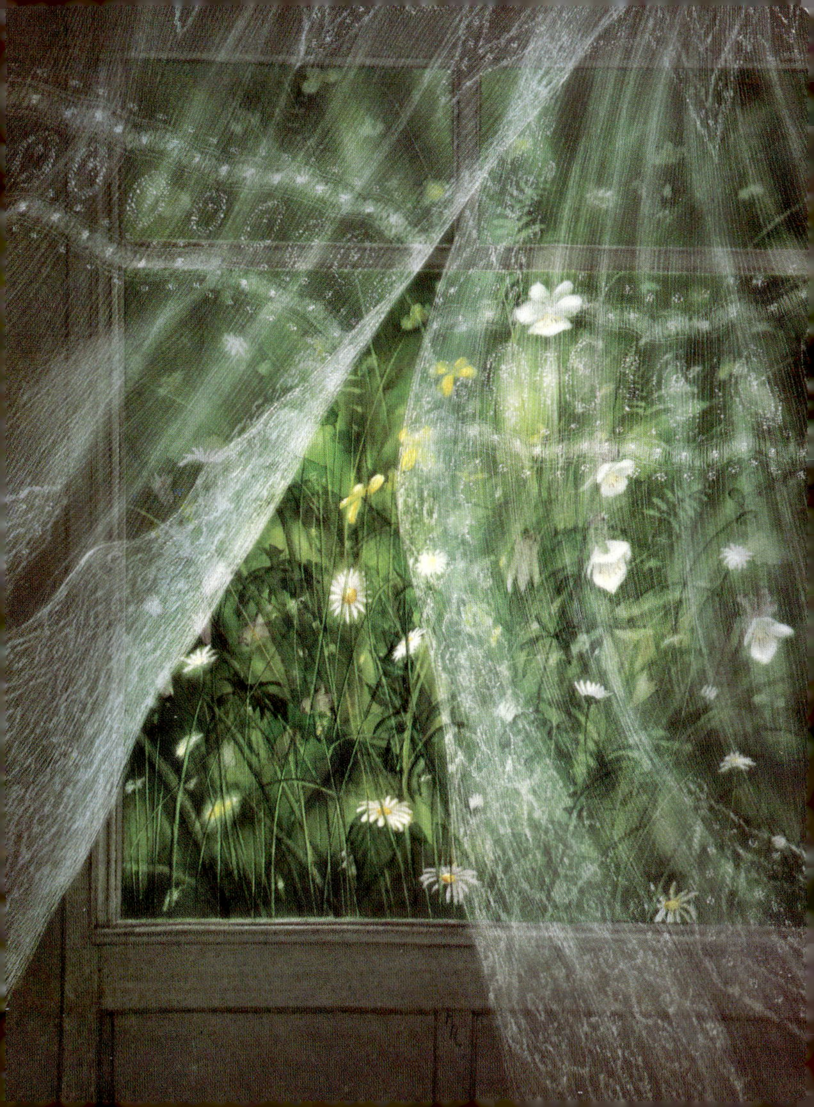

1/1



The Blue Ribbon/ Das blaue Band

Bluestar Communications
Woodside, California
800-6-BLUESTAR

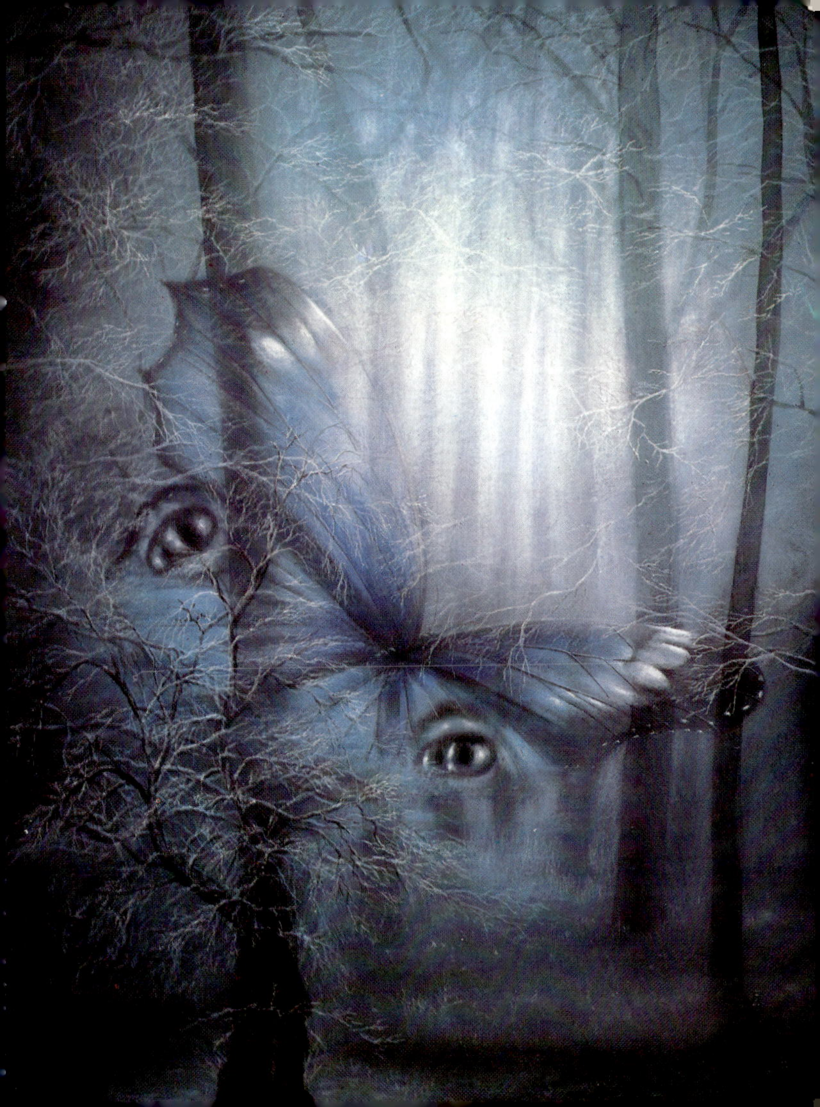

1/2



Winter Chorale/ Winterchoral

Bluestar Communications
Woodside, California
800-6-BLUESTAR

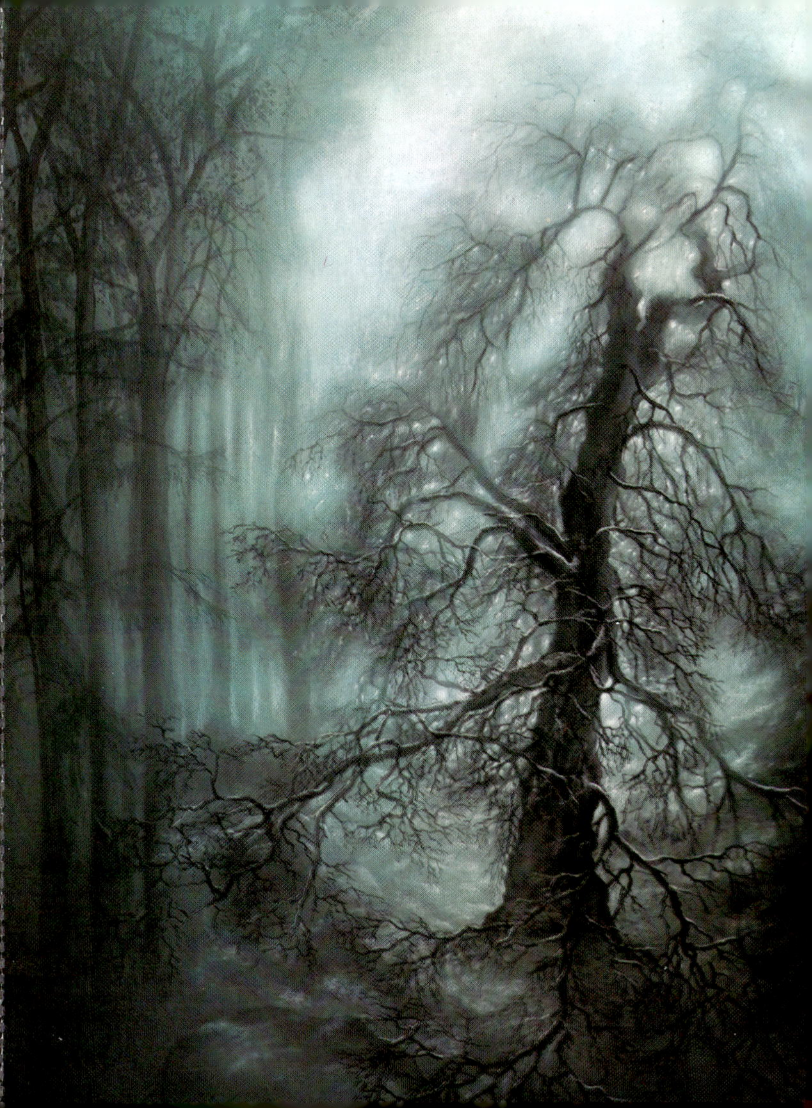

1/3



The Tired Pasture/ Die schläfrige Aue

Bluestar Communications
Woodside, California
800-6-BLUESTAR

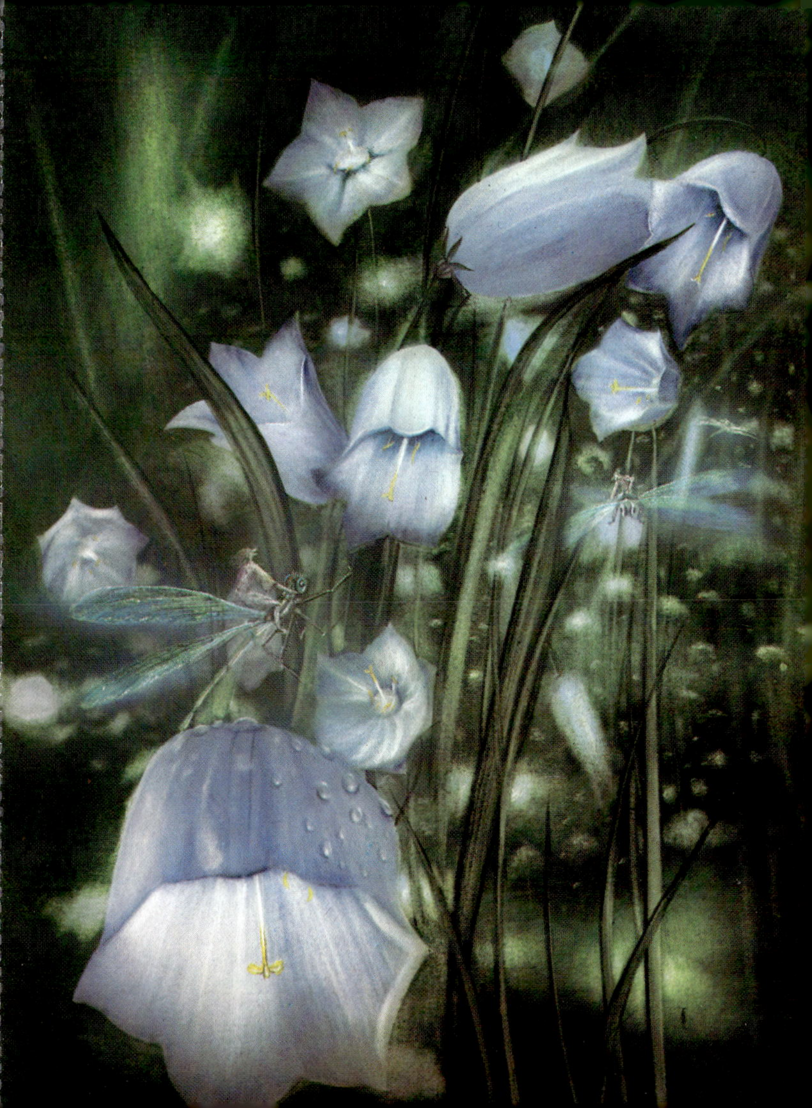

1/4



The First Outing/ Der erste Ausflug

Bluestar Communications
Woodside, California
800-6-BLUESTAR

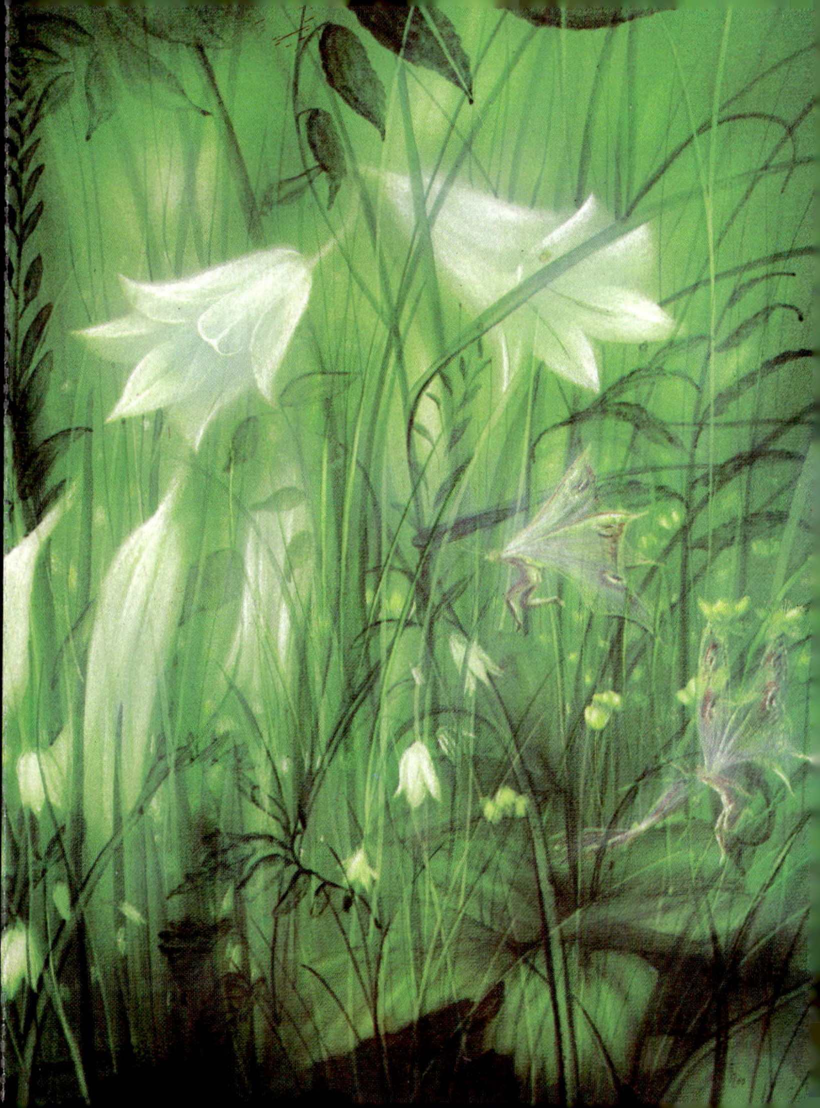

1/5



Midsummer Night's Dream/ Sommernachtstraum

Bluestar Communications
Woodside, California
800-6-BLUESTAR

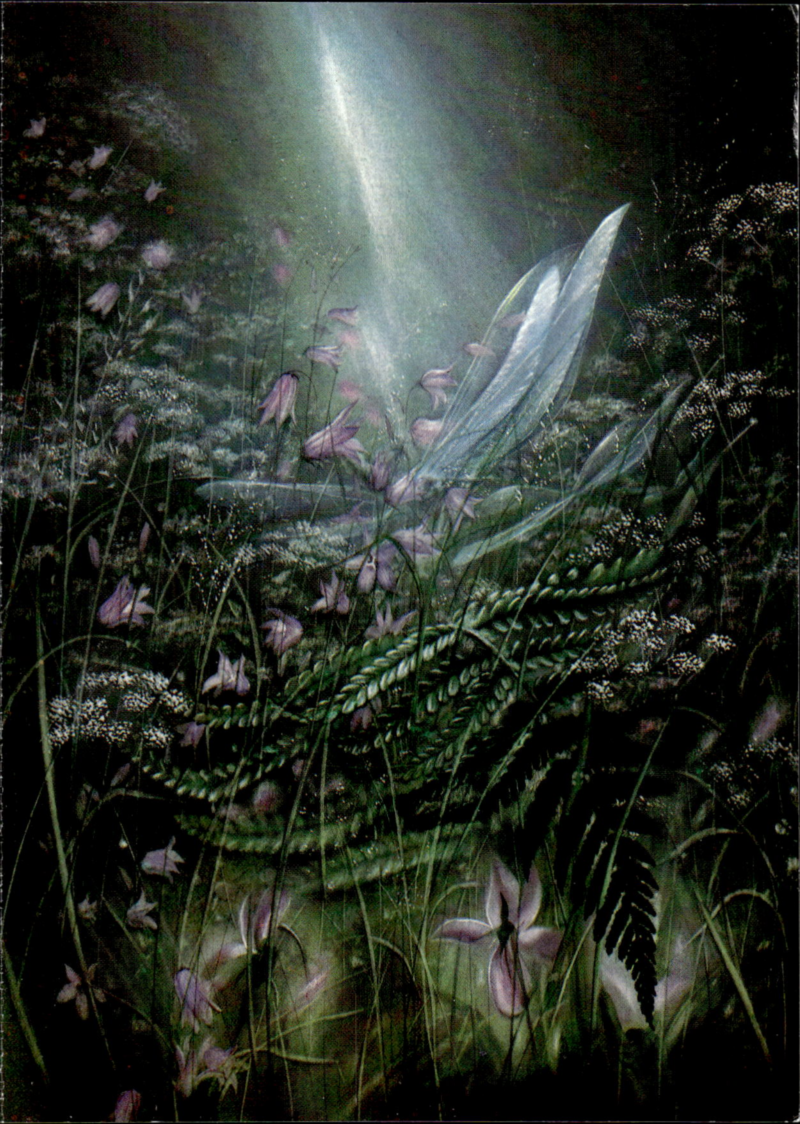

1/6



The Hidden Aura/ Die verborgene Aura

Bluestar Communications
Woodside, California
800-6-BLUESTAR

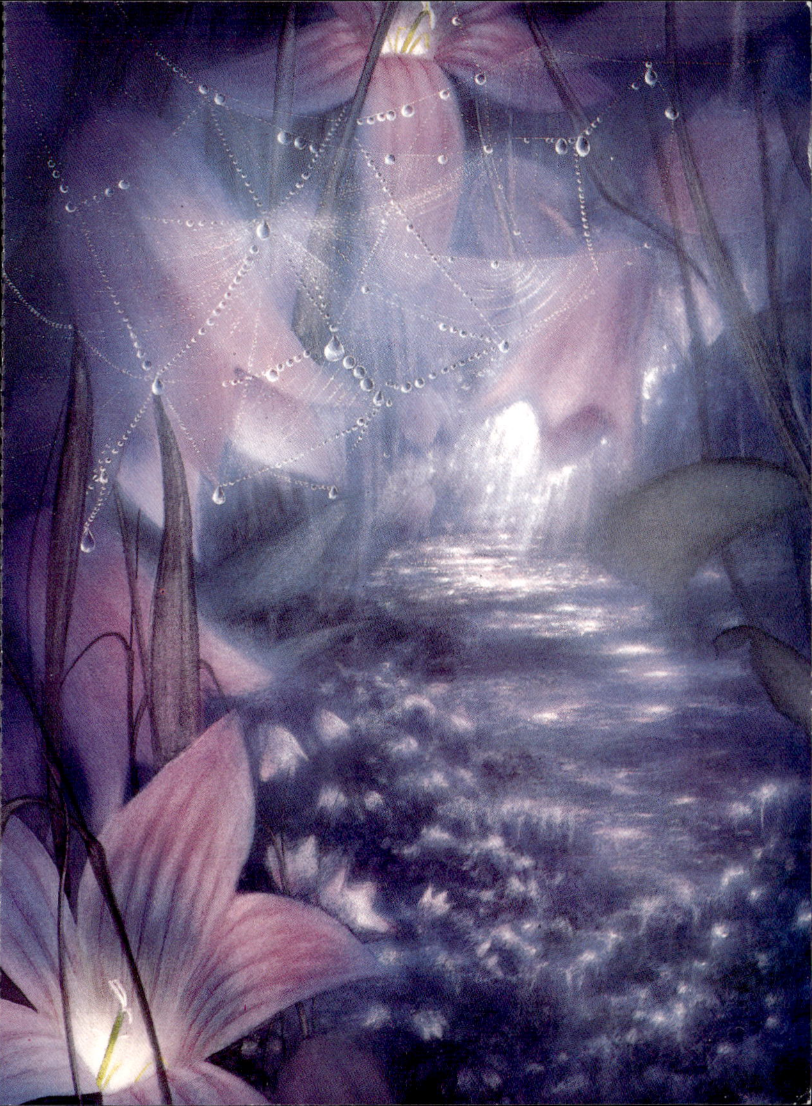

1/7



The Forgotten Weavers/ Die vergessenen Weber

Bluestar Communications
Woodside, California
800-6-BLUESTAR

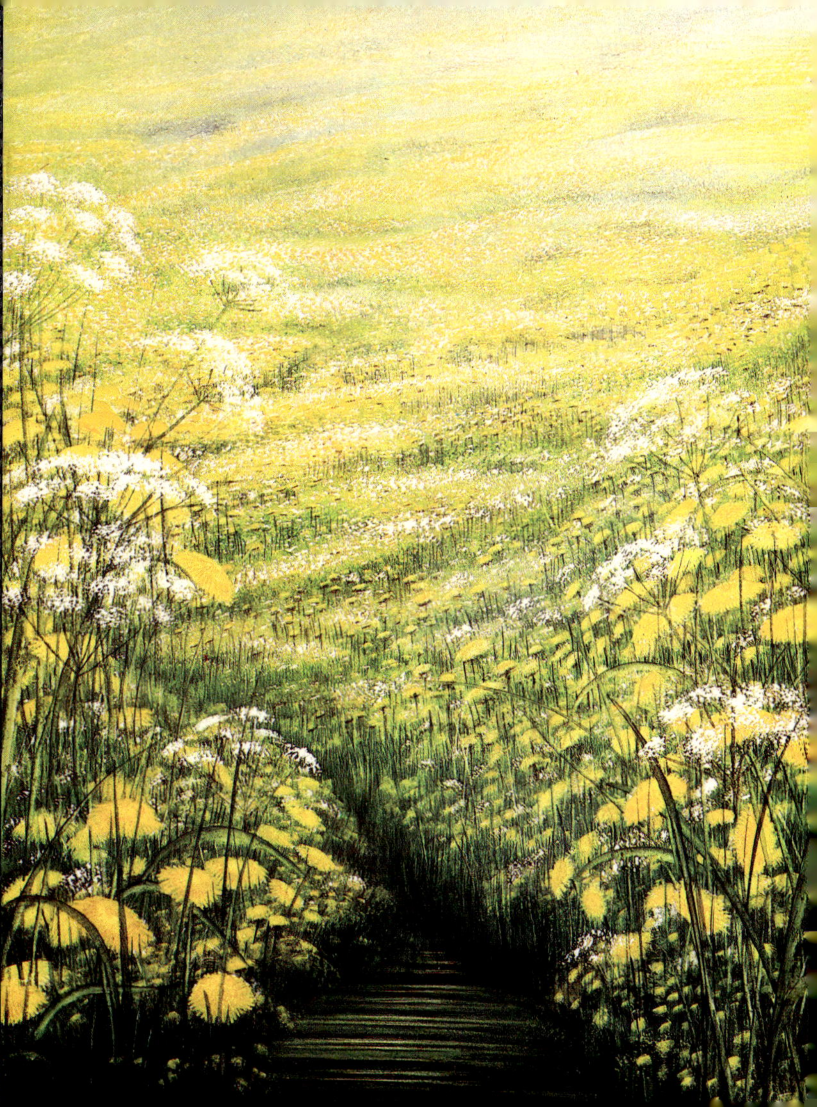

1/8



Scene for Ballet/ Szenenbild für Ballettverfilmung

Bluestar Communications
Woodside, California
800-6-BLUESTAR

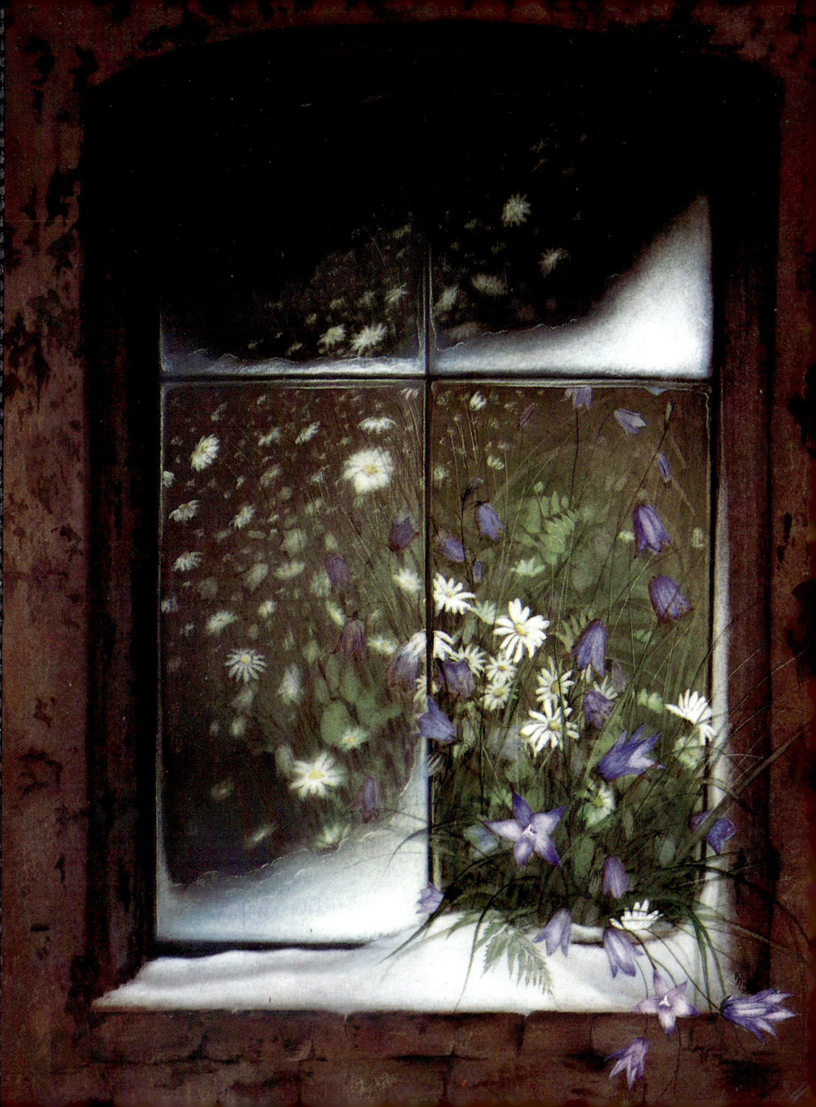

1/9



Caprice

Bluestar Communications
Woodside, California
800-6-BLUESTAR

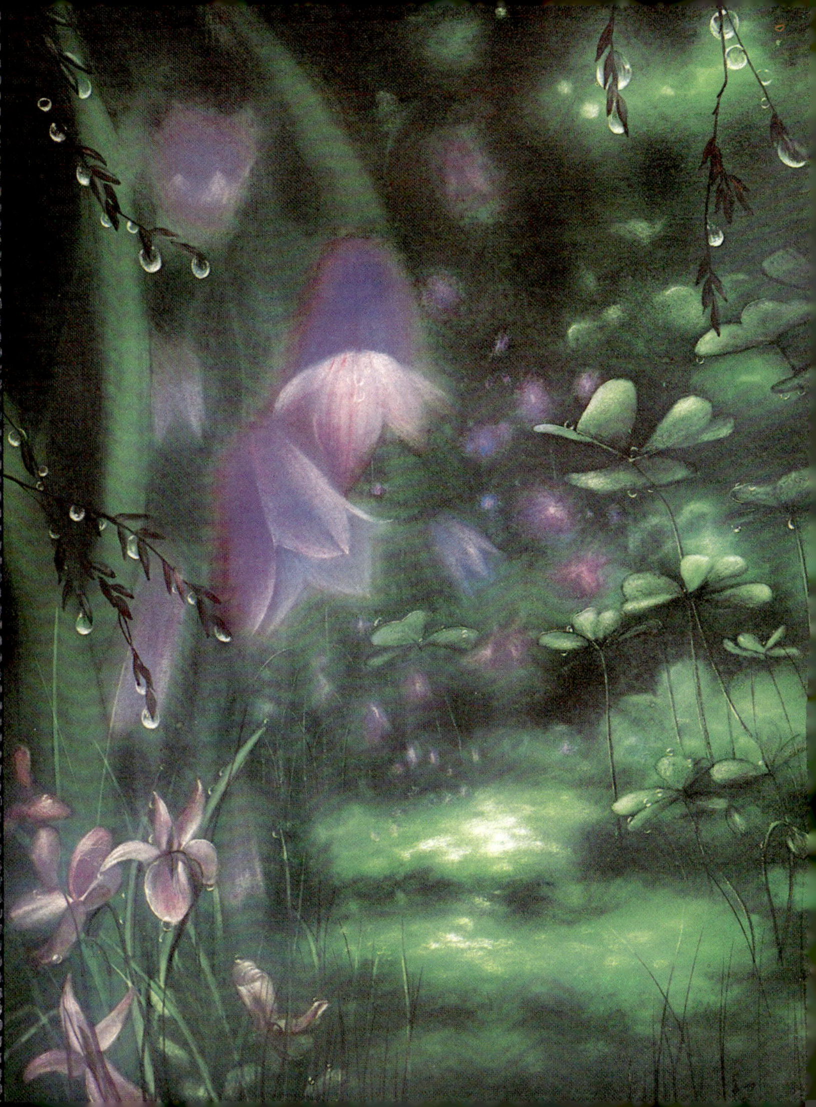

1/10



Scene for Ballet/ Szenenbild für Ballettverfilmung

Bluestar Communications
Woodside, California
800-6-BLUESTAR

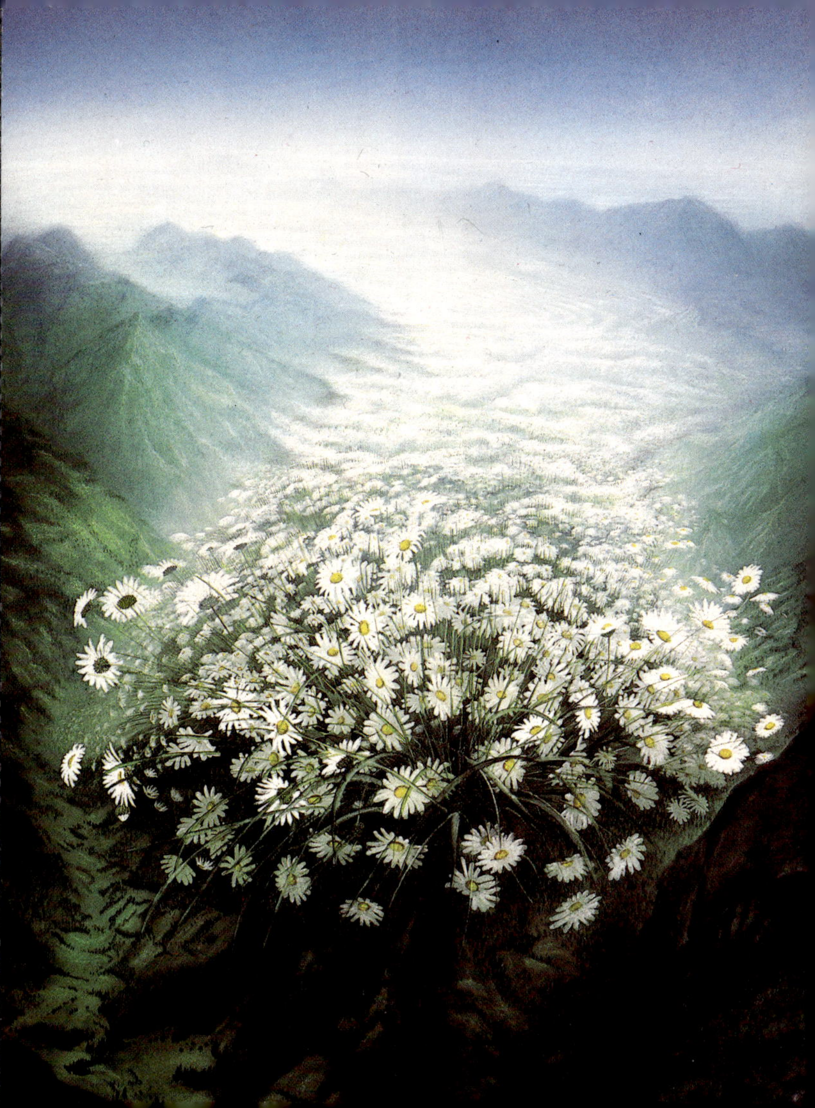

1/11



First Song/ Erster Gesang

Bluestar Communications
Woodside, California
800-6-BLUESTAR

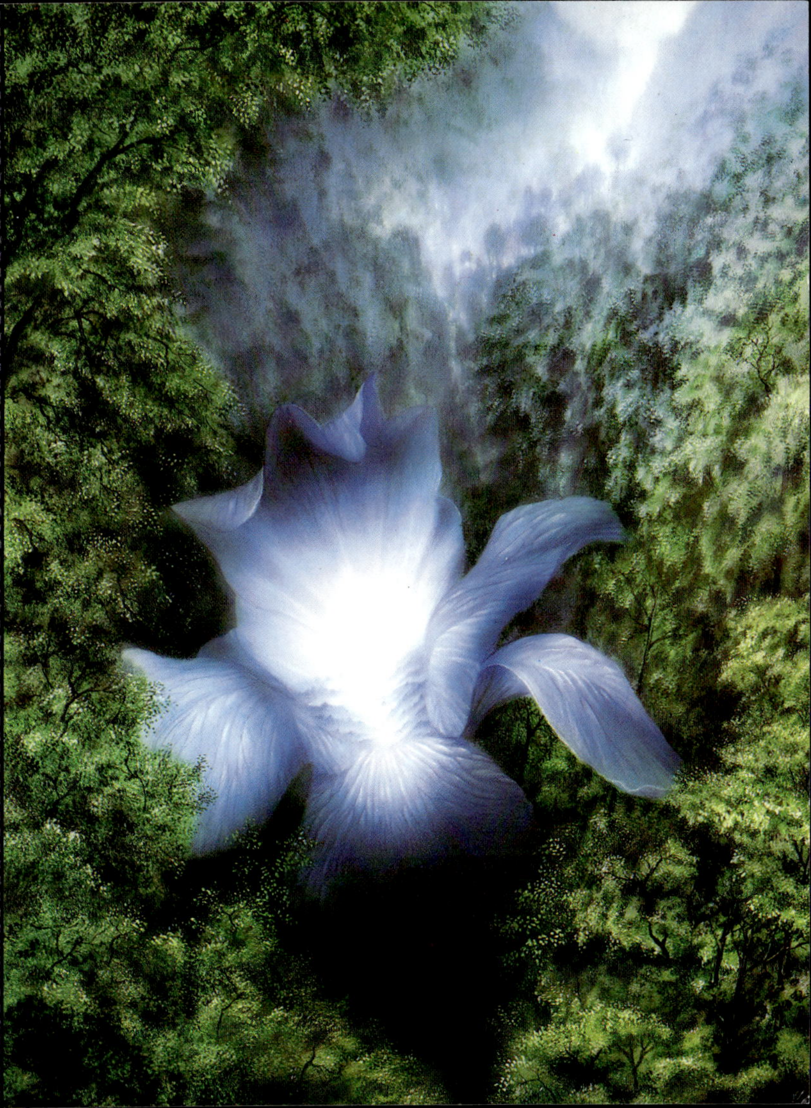

1/12



Self-Communion/ Die Einkehr

Bluestar Communications
Woodside, California
800-6-BLUESTAR

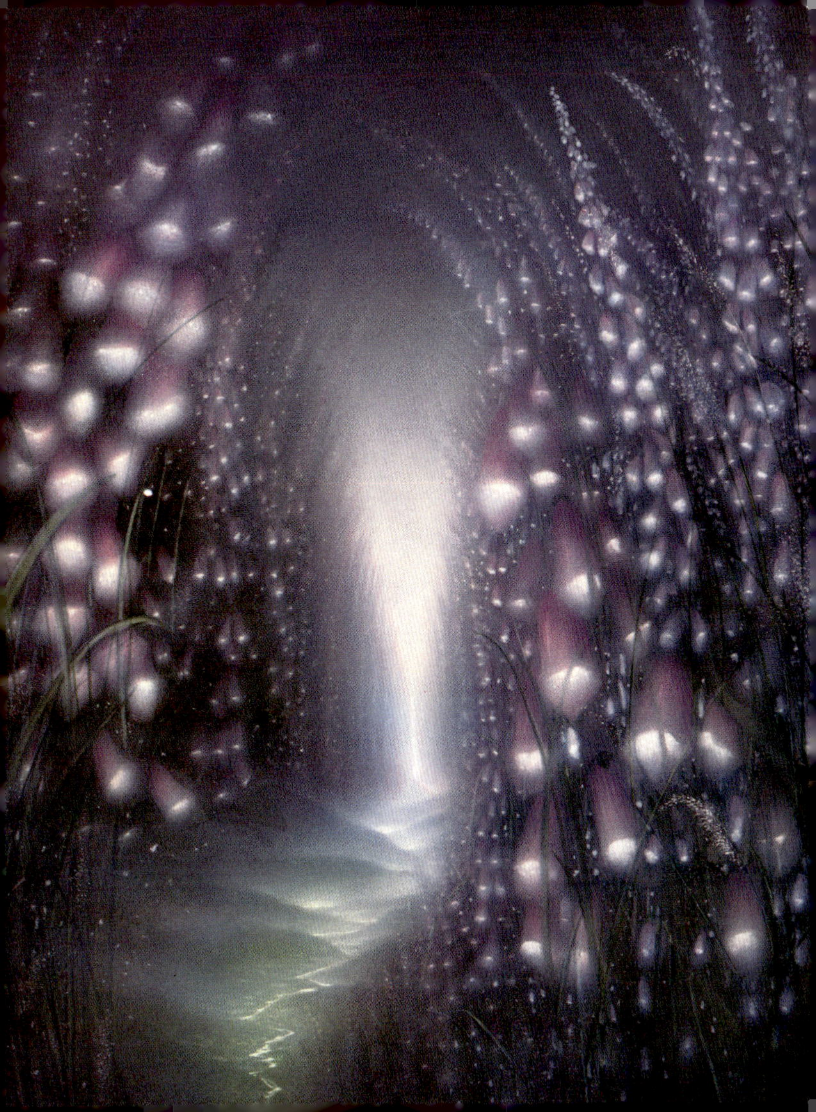

1/13



Alley/ Allee

Bluestar Communications
Woodside, California
800-6-BLUESTAR

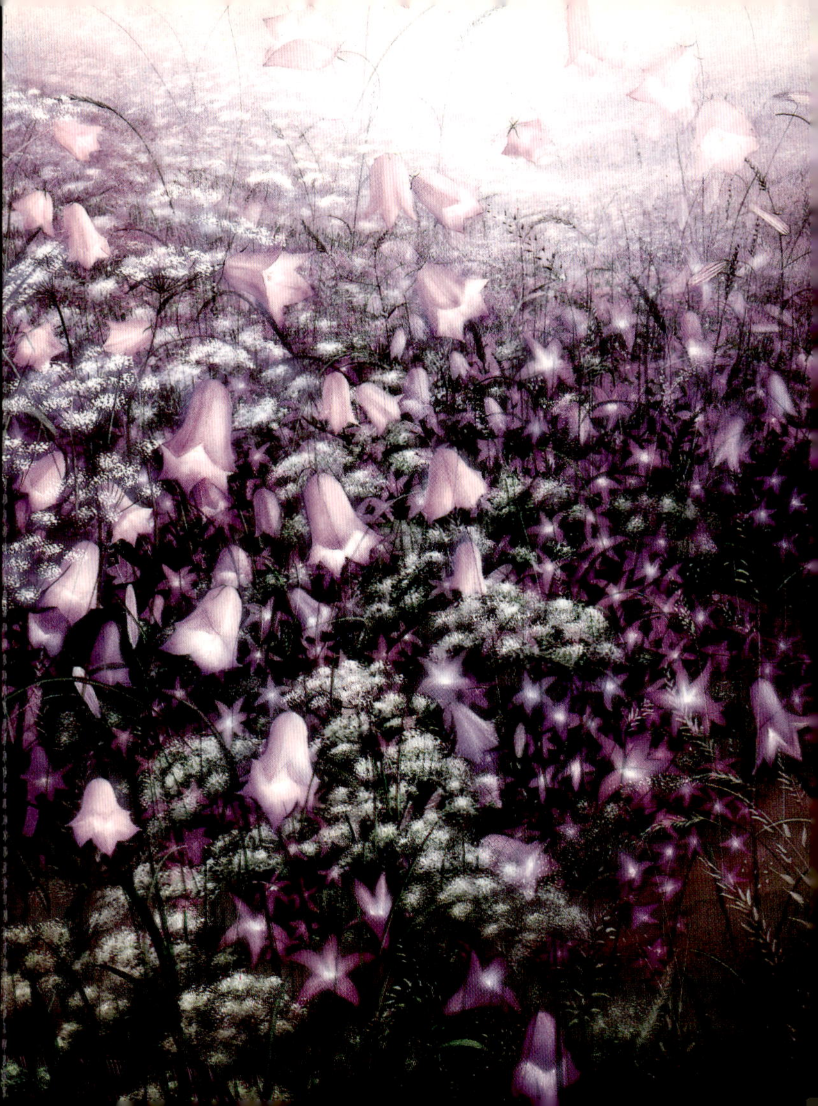

1/14



Campanula

Bluestar Communications
Woodside, California
800-6-BLUESTAR

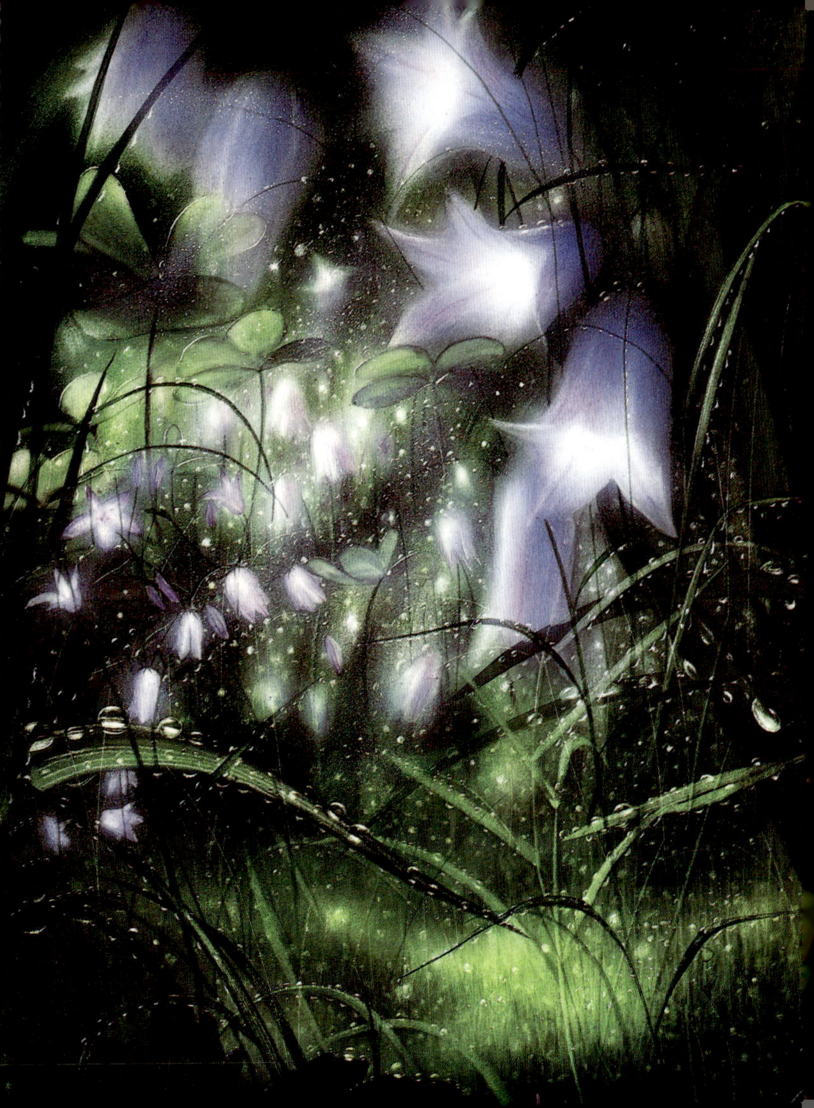

1/15



Scene for Ballet/ Szenenbild für Ballettverfilmung

Bluestar Communications
Woodside, California
800-6-BLUESTAR

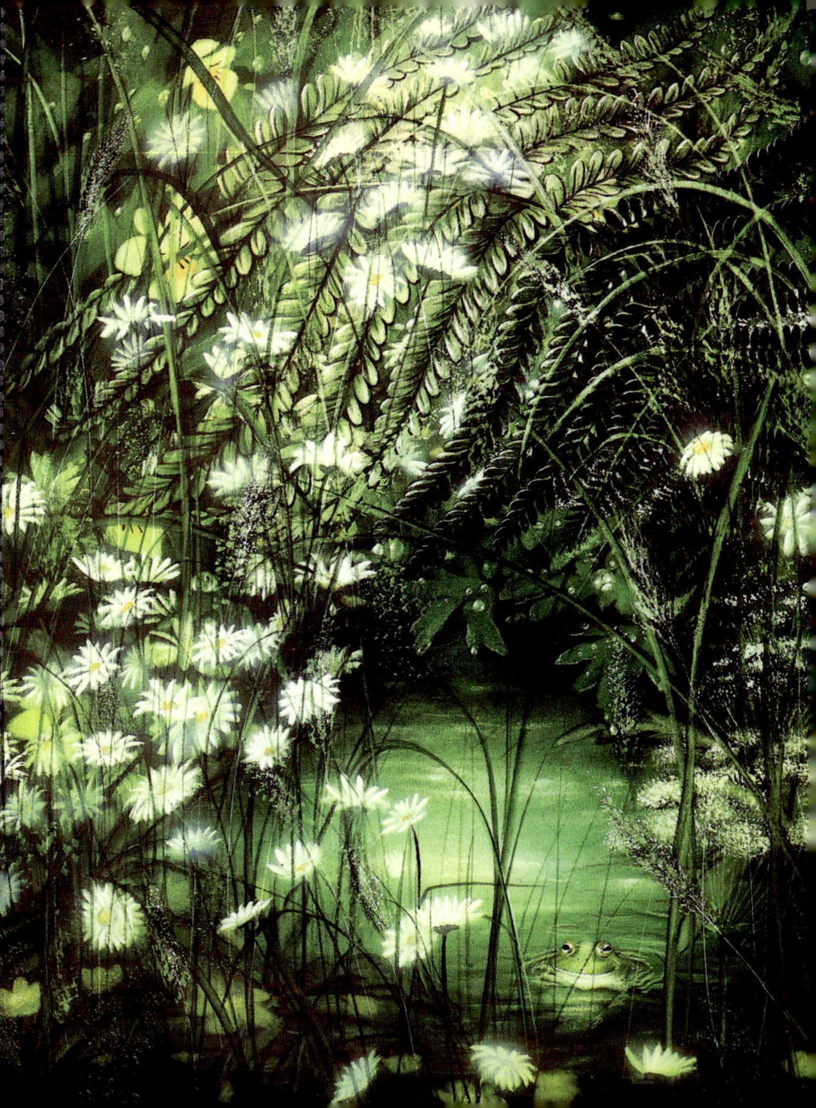

1/16



From: Hechelmann's Bilder-Buch zum Schreiben

Bluestar Communications
Woodside, California
800-6-BLUESTAR

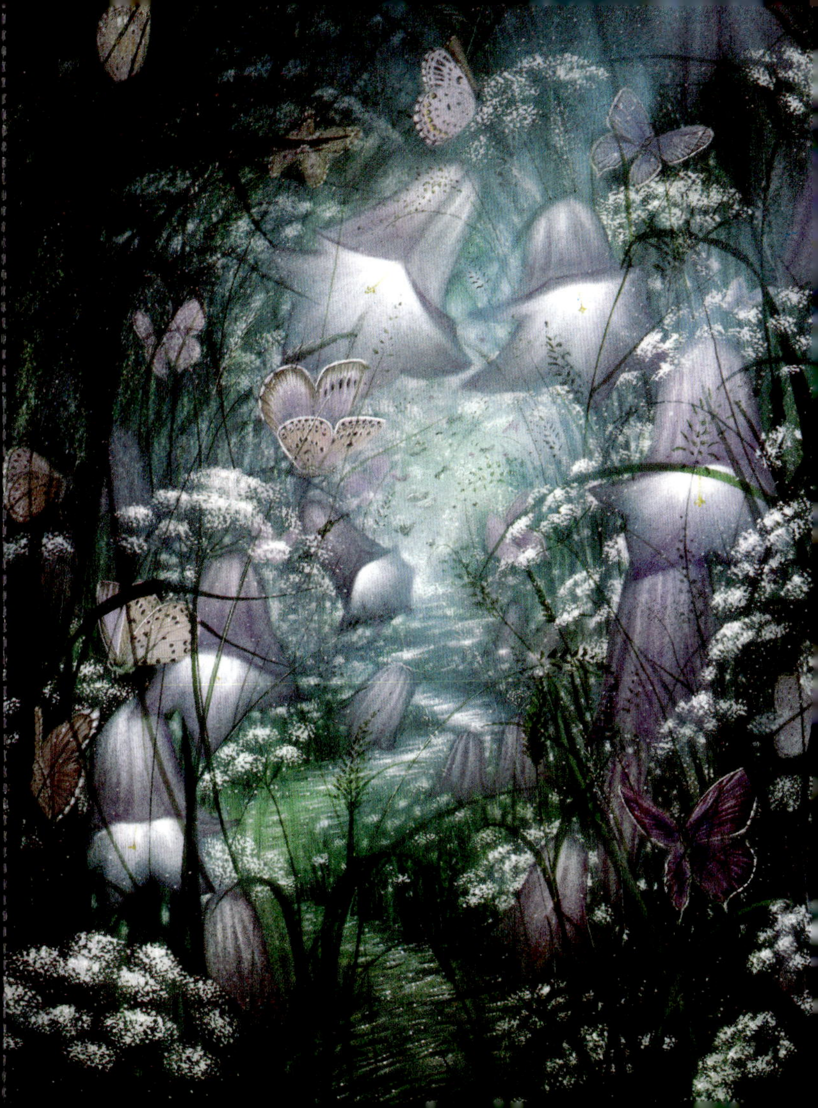

1/17



From: Hechelmann's Bilder-Buch zum Schreiben

Bluestar Communications
Woodside, California
800-6-BLUESTAR

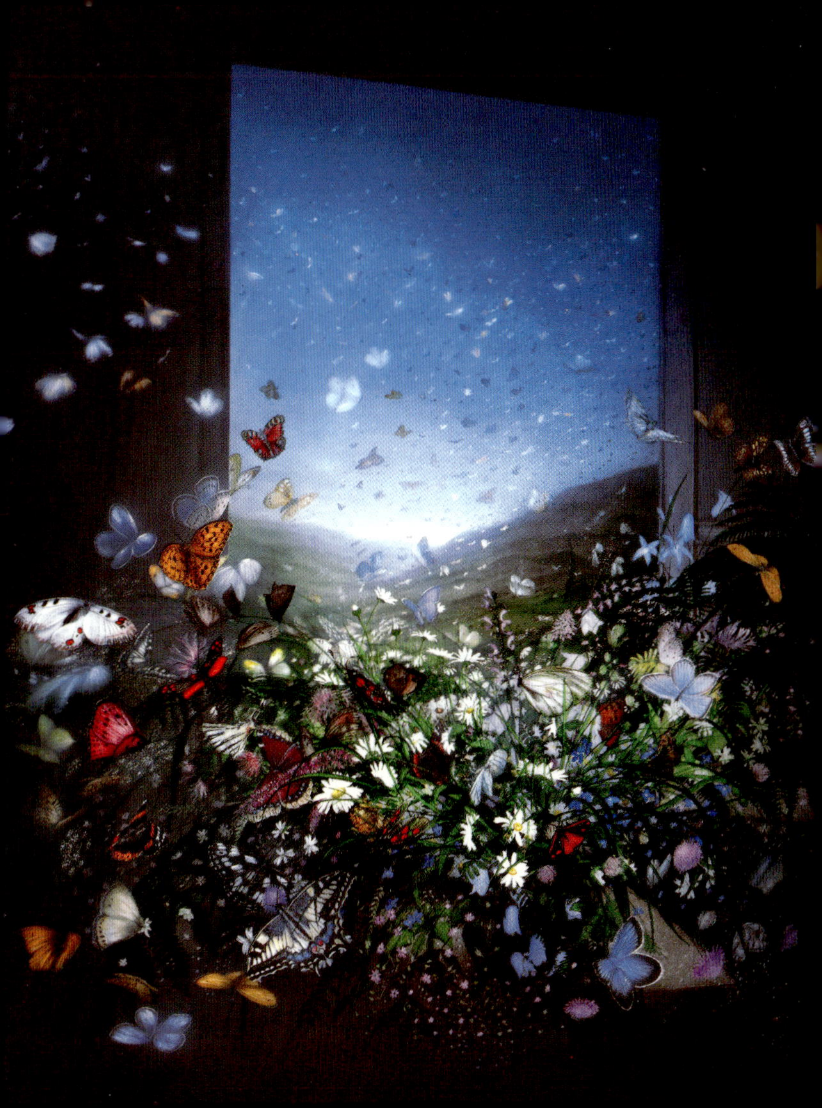

1/18



The Big Roundelay/ Großer Reigen

Bluestar Communications
Woodside, California
800-6-BLUESTAR

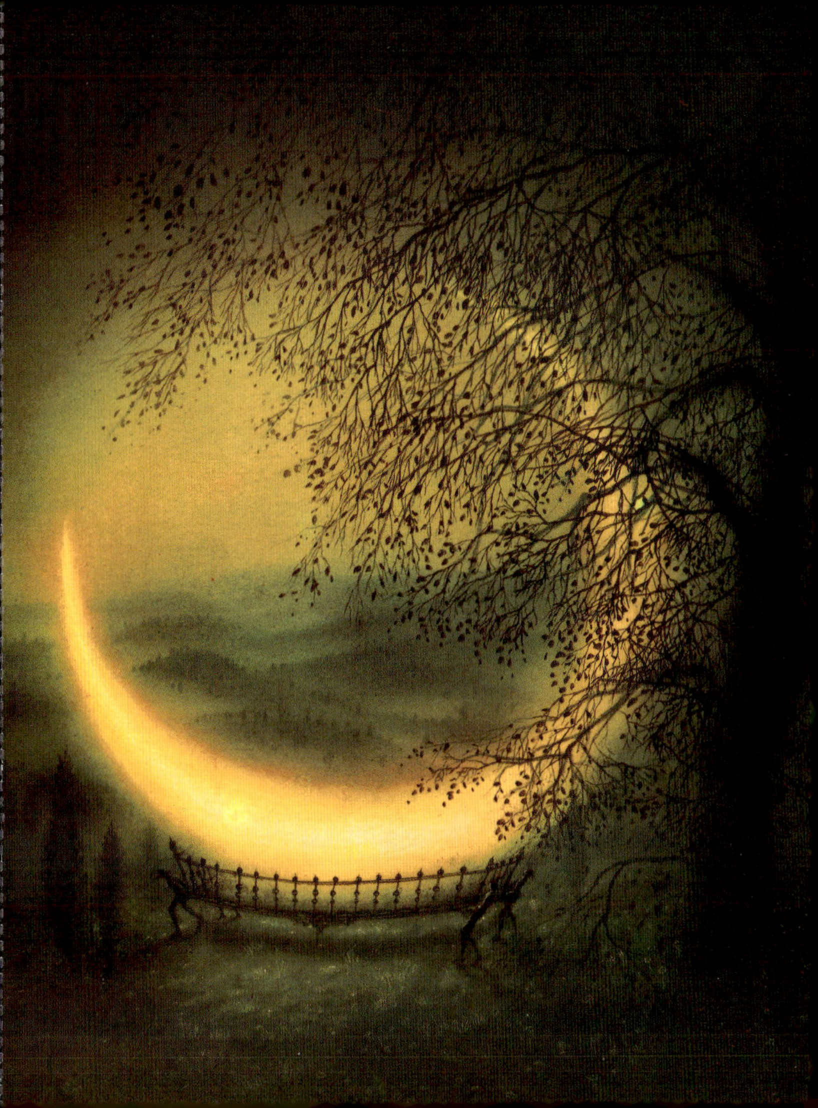

1/19



Untitled

Bluestar Communications
Woodside, California
800-6-BLUESTAR